Touching All the Bases

Touching All the Bases

Poems from Baseball

by
TIM PEELER

Prologue by J. L. Peeler

McFarland & Company, Inc., Publishers
Jefferson, North Carolina, and London

Acknowledgments

The author wishes to offer thanks to these publications in which the following poems first appeared: *Aethlon*: "When I First Saw Feller Pitch"; *Enteractive Weekly:* "Nobody Ever Stole," "It Makes You Scratch Your Head," "Sometimes You've Got to Change the Names," "John Wayneing," "The Thing About Terry," "Running in LP Frans Stadium," "The Rainbow Kid Remembers Little League"; *A Carolina Literary Companion:* "Gaylord"; *Jean's Journal:* "Adirondack"; *Pig in a Poke*: "Spikes and Leather"; and *Spitball*. "Curt Flood," "whiskey moon," "Mr. October Came to Catawba County," "Baseball Angel," "An Asterisk as Big as a Ball," "Henry Louis," "Aaron," "The Walls of Comiskey," "Budweiser!" "The Catcher Learns the Motion," "Josh as I Am," "The Babe Ruth Syndrome," "Josh, What the Future," "Josh, in the Islands," "Baseball Archeologists," "Charlie Pitchback," "The Fall I Bet My Lunch Money," "How Coffey Got His Nerves," "Touching All the Bases," "Yaz at the Hall," "Jim Rice Viewing the Fenway Wall," "Concepción," "Summer of '85," Holding Back, "So I've Got the Class," "Writing Baseball Poems in Winter," "When Dizzy," "When Wolfe Watched the Dodgers," "Baseball Haiku I," "Baseball Haiku II," "Banks," "Neikro Summoning Paige, 1987," "Radio Seasons," "Atlanta Stadium — View from the Blue Seats," "My Ten Year Old Said," and "Extra Innings." "Curt Flood" has also appeared in two anthologies: *The Best of Spitball*, Pocket Books; and *Hummers, Knucklers, and Curveballs*, University of Illinois Press.

Library of Congress Cataloguing-in-Publication Data are available

ISBN 0-7864-0705-0 (softcover : 50# acid-free paper) ∞

British Library Cataloguing-in-Publication data are available

Manufactured in the United States of America

McFarland & Company, Inc., Publishers
  Box 611, Jefferson, North Carolina 28640
  www.mcfarlandpub.com

To the memory of Cooke Mull, Frank Murphy,
and Steve "The Rainbow Kid" Lail

For my wife, Penny, who inspires me,
For my dad, who still coaches me, and, most of all,
For my brother Paul, who shared a childhood of baseball

CONTENTS

PREFACE

My experience with baseball literature began a long time before my involvement with it as a writer. In fact, that early experience is intrinsically tied together with my love for the game itself. When I was in the third grade, I read a biography about Hank Aaron. I had read a number of such bios, along with juvenile sports fiction by people like Matt Christopher. But nothing moved me like this story of a young black man who rose from a humble existence in Mobile, Alabama, to become one of the game's great players. Coincidentally, the Milwaukee Braves moved to Atlanta that same year and Aaron became a sports icon in the South. I had been playing baseball since I was six, but that year, 1966, I became a fan of the game.

Like most of the consequential incidents in my life, I came across the world of baseball poetry quite by accident. I had after college, in the early 1980s, begun writing (especially poetry) in earnest. By 1982 I was regularly sending work out to the small press literary magazines that serve as a kind of undergirding for the literary scene in the United States. In one such magazine I discovered a review for a small magazine that specifically published baseball-related poetry and fiction. I had soon sent my first offering to Mike Shannon at *Spitball: The Literary Baseball Magazine*. The first poem I sent was the title poem for this book, "Touching All the Bases."

For fifteen years I continued sporadically to dip my pen in horsehide ink. Much of this work found its way into Shannon's lively publication. Over time Mike offered a great deal of encouragement and moral support. Although the baseball poetry was only a small part of my writing, I returned to it again and again as a respite and an enjoyment. And though I found other outlets for my work, *Spitball* had the sense of humor, comfort level and the sheer gravity to bring me back. It was and is the first home to many of the poems in this book. And in that space, I learned to appreciate the work of others dedicated to the craft of baseball poetry. Robert Harrison, Gene Fehler, Jim Palana, and Jan Brodt were some of the names that I came to expect and admire in Shannon's magazine.

Two significant events occurred regarding my avocation as a writer in 1998. First, through another random act of good fortune I began writing regularly for a local weekly entertainment tabloid called *Enteractive Weekly*. The publisher, David Nelson, gave me almost complete editorial freedom with the essays, poems, and interviews that I submitted. Writing for *EA* and keeping up with other freelance opportunities instilled a greater sense of discipline in my work and work ethic. This discipline would prove very important to the completion of the manuscript for this book, for when I submitted it to McFarland, only 80 of the 130 poems had been written.

The remaining 50 were accomplished over a four week period, a time during which I learned a great deal about myself. What I discovered during that month was that if you have a sufficient love for the craft and your subject matter, it is possible to come to the word processor nightly, even with a heavy work schedule, to chase the splendor and joy of your past through line after line of energized and often cathartic effort. Some nights you must begin with no more than the pitcher's faith to throw the curve on a 3–0 count. Other nights you sit down with enough intensity to light the park with a new idea.

Although the manuscript came together in this manner, the order of the book's content in no way reflects the "old" versus the "newer" poems. In fact, the newer ones are interspersed, hopefully in a seamless manner. While my ability to conceive and execute a poem may have improved, the accessible style and narrative candor have remained the same.

It is and has always been my intention to reach people through the subject of sport who might not ordinarily connect with poetry. If this happens, then I will have succeeded. At any rate, with the publication of this volume, I invite you into my life. I wish to share with you my friends, my family, my past and present competitors, my heroes, my curiosities, and most of all, the splendor and the joy of my memories.

Prologue by J. L. Peeler, the Poet's Father

The following prologue was originally written in early 1991 as an introduction to my chapbook of poems, Swing at Every Pitch. *I hope the reader will agree that it still provides a helpful generational link to my interest in the game.*

I was so young when I became interested in baseball. I cannot remember exactly when my love affair started. The first thing I recall is trying to make baseballs out of the threads unraveled from an old sock. If you could find a small rubber ball and some black tape, you could make a very good "baseball," but small rubber balls and tape were both very scarce on a red dirt farm in Rowan County, N.C., in the early 1930s, and so were playmates since my older brothers spent most of their time tilling the soil.

In view of the scarcity of baseballs I used substitutes. My favorites were green apples and rocks. In the summer I would spend hours at a time hitting and throwing. I got to the place I could put an impressive curve on an apple, but no one else knew about it or cared about it.

As I got a little older, I dreamed of getting up a community team to play other nearby communities. Naturally, I would be the pitcher and the coach. However, there were only three or four other boys in the area. I did succeed in getting up one game, "a classic" with Rowan Mills. By this time (about fifth grade) I had managed to get a catcher's mitt. I thought this was the only equipment we needed besides a few homemade bats.

We managed to get only four or five players there, but we "played." I didn't get to pitch (for which I thought I was trained) nor did I get to coach. There were not enough players to be coached. What I had to do was catch because no one else would do it. Without any kind of protection and no experience, it was horrible. We got beaten as badly as Charlie Brown's team. This cured me from ever trying to catch again, but it did not dim my love affair with baseball.

I must have been in the seventh grade when I learned about the major leagues. Since we had no radio and could not afford a newspaper, I had a difficult time keeping up with what was going on. You know the old saying, "Love will find a way." I did find a way. My neighbor's mailbox was beside ours and he received the daily paper by mail. Each day after the mail came, I would sneak the paper out and hastily read the baseball news. As far as I know, neither my parents nor my neighbor ever discovered my secret.

In this manner I learned about Hank Greenberg's homerun hitting and Johnny Vandermeer's successive no-hitters. Thus my love for the game reached new heights of passion. In the next few years, after my older brothers began to work at the dairy farm located a half mile from home, I was treated to a new privilege. Music was considered good for cows, so my neighbor installed a radio in the milking barn. He allowed one or two days a week to listen to baseball games on the radio. I was introduced to the Washington Senators games. Other games could not be heard in the South. The announcer's name was Hodges (I have forgotten his first name) and he broadcast by ticker tape. The Senators were comparable to today's Atlanta Braves, perennial losers, but the announcer made their games exciting. It was in that same dairy barn I heard my first World Series game. What excitement that was!

During this period in my life, I often daydreamed about being a Major League pitcher and I still practiced, with a real baseball now. When I could get someone to catch me. My high school was located five miles away. Since I had no means of transportation, I could not play on the team. I did take my mitt and ball to school. Once during recess I was pitching to my best friend, who was not very athletic. As I warmed up, I began to throw the ball hard. Soon he missed one of my speed balls and I thought I had seriously injured him for life.

Since I never fulfilled my dream, I thought one of my sons would become a pitcher. The youngest one started playing organized ball at age 5 and had a strong arm from the beginning. I was often his coach and his practice catcher in the backyard. I would never let him overuse his arm. He did become an exceptional pitcher with an easy motion, a sharp curve and a good fastball, but by the time he got into high school he began to lose interest and never pitched beyond the junior varsity level.

Today, one of his greatest interests is writing poetry, I wanted him to become a pitcher. He became a poet. But, believe it or not, he has re-kindled his love for baseball, and is probably North Carolina's best known baseball poet.

As for me, the Lord called me to be a preacher of the Gospel. After forty plus years, I still love people and I minister to the most helpless as Chaplain of the Lutheran Home in Hickory, N.C., but none of this has destroyed my not so secret love of baseball.

As long as I have ability to comprehend, I will be thrilled by such things as a Nolan Ryan no-hitter, a Cecil Fielder home run, even an occasional win by the Braves. And someday, just maybe I will see one of my grandsons pitching a Major League game (unless they become poets or preachers).

J. L. Peeler
The Poet's Father
September 1991

Curt Flood

try to tell 'em Curt,
how you crowned their wallets,
climbed courtroom steps
for them,
swallowed that black ball,
a scapegoat out to pasture.
they don't remember,
can't remember
the trash you ate,
your greedy headlines,
the slope of your career.

you are a ghost at barterer's wing,
your smoky gray eyes
are two extra zeroes
on every contract.

Swing at Every Pitch

My oldest son
has a Dale Murphy swing
I feed it
fifteen year old horsehide
Jamaican stitched
the last ball Dad gave me
before reefer
sucked the promise
right out of my curve
when my hair hung like Pepi-
tone's
yes Pepitone
remember the Ringo Starr
of baseball

Now I am the dreamer
Grin and Buy
the sweet small percentage
Pitch and field the torch

My son circles popups
under a flame of red hair
I watch him carelessly
wonder will he also
swing at every pitch

When I First Saw Feller Pitch

I knew man was headed somewhere he hadn't been,
for when the pocket of the mitt exploded
you'd swear the pitch had whistled like a firework fuse
that held your anticipating breath,
then sprinkled bright stars against its dark report,
and you knew that somehow rocket travel
would soon be possible,
that gravity had begun to lose its clutch
on our physical imagination
and we were nearly ready to move on out
into the perilous night.

First At-Bat

a strong whiff of freshly cut grass
cocks memory's trigger,
fires me back
to the peewee league ball field,
sucks my small head
inside the funny, half-shell helmet
with stretched elastic band across
the top,
much too big and my thick,
black-rimmed
glasses will not stay up,
a whole ocean of summer air
swirls through seashell ear holes,

dads and moms are restless
on the warped slats of cracked
bleachers
cooped there behind the chicken
wire backstop
through five eternal innings of
walks
and strikeouts.

jetstreams of cotton
crisscross overhead.
the thundering lawnmower
on the next field over
spews a strong, green whiff
of fresh grass
as I tremble toward the plate.

whiskey moon

frank says the full moon
is for whiskey,
spits tobacco to punctuate
his short sentences,
hours sipping, replaying
his career in slow motion,
oiling the first baseman's mitt,
then spreading it carefully
to catch the milky light,
frank says it softens the leather,
I say it embalms the memory.

The Emperor of Baseball

(with apologies to Wallace Stevens)

Call the brewer of kingly beer,
The affluent one, bid him build
A team and field fleet and smooth.
Let Huck's river run near and slow as a
Look through arch westward at
A stadium dressed in shirt sleeves in early fall.
The only emperor is the emperor of baseball.

Take from the islands their human yield,
Lacking but in poverty there, that outfield
On which they will scoot is embroidered
With memories that spread to cover
The speedy bats of the past.
In record books mercurial feet protrude.
Let the great ghost of Gibson
Affix its awesome beam of fastball.
The only emperor is the emperor of baseball.

If Cobb Could See Ozzie's Cardinals, 1985

He'd buy a season ticket,
Maybe the whole crazy club —
Change the name to Coca-Cola Stadium,
Curse the other teams'
Home Run hitters
With a gruff old goat voice
And a boxseat cigar.
They'd all hate him for being such a bastard,
And a rich one,
Patronize him with an opening game first toss,
Finally, respect him
When he shut up
And got down to talking the game.

Charlie Hustle Is Linking for You

The line is inexplicably busy —
He was promised high-speed modem easy access —
Finally, he breaks through the glut
With the persistence of speed dial and the gambler's
Intuition of when to click —

The colors, the numbers, the screens all
Flip by and slip by as he mouse powers
With the same stodgy finger
That once shook in an umpire's deep red face —
Ten, fifteen years ago, he couldn't have done this —
Couldn't have suffered a claustrophobic moment
Answering the e-mail at peterose.com
Or scrolled down to search for another detail
About Ty Cobb's theory on hitting —
He would have busted open and busted the screen
Or slammed the keyboard into the wall
Waiting for a download or tomorrow's weather —

Now the color shifts to a rich burgundy and
There he is back at the Hall of Fame site,
Entering a door that can't shut down his anonymous
Electronic urge to be there.

Nobody Ever Stole

like Lou Brock;
say what you will about your Henderson,
your Cobb, your Wills;
Brock went like the slash of a knife.
Baseball, track, and poker met
in the cool shift of his eyes;
the agitated pitcher peered
over his left shoulder — a weak hand of cards
against this Card — who led
so brassy and distant from the sack —
whose acrobatics made him safe
from the surest gunslinging cowboys —
who only stole when he needed,
no ninth inning ten run lead prima donna —
NOBODY EVER STOLE
like Lou Brock
on the high wire of a tenth inning tie
so incredibly
and so often.

Mr. October Came to Catawba County

four barrel SS Chevelle 396
for those numbers he jetted
like a long drive from CA
like the howitzer shot
in that Detroit All-Star game
beyond the flat line of vision

for the great eight cylinder redneck growl
like his own unmuffled swing,
Reggie in retirement came
to Catawba County, to
Blue Ridge foothills not noble
jagged rocky western mountains, rather soft
and rolling like a plump herd of hogs
lying down in red clay

to replace his houseburned collection
of muscle cars — not one
to pile regret upon regret —
Mr. October in ripe Southern September
came to Catawba County
and local good old boy tv commercial
used car dealer
realized the pecuniary salvation
for his ragshine worship Saturday afternoons
and sacred engine tune midnights,
built a big new lot yessiree
with his share of Jackson

chauffeured Big Apple/California Reggie
to a high school football game
ended in a circle of little black kids
hungry for a mild word of acknowledgement

"Hey Mista Octoba! Hey Mista Octoba!"
the chant that circled and marched on its own power
till finally with certainty
he knew just where the heck he wuz.

Baseball Angel

she has a ballpark figure —
deep in center field,
shallow at the corners —
her new blue jeans are
a crowded sellout —
dugout pockets,
foul line seams.
two carefully contoured mounds,
one in each bullpen.

The Cycle

Sin and Repentance,
the absolute whirlygig swing
reeling to a knee —
big white cat circling the sacks,
Sin and Repentance,
the circuit teeming
with "parties to see,"
nights to cook slowly, foamy beer
to slosh and curfews to belch,
a sun to greet in its first blister —
Sin and Repentance,
man-god strength to propel
salaries, fans,
and baseballs up
and glory high on "the wheel" —
frontpage headline newsreel high —
you had to be there high,
Sin and Repentance,
the awkward husband, father,
in a twirl of fast seasons
dashing away in Black Packard
madness,
Florida golfer,
Hot Springs to unpork,
Sin and Repentance,
another blurring swing,
his father
horsewhipping the boy
that stole a dollar from the saloon till
to buy ice cream for his buddies —
took it
and took another.

When You're About to Shatter a Myth

(for Roger Maris, 1934–85)

The jealous will always be there,
Praying for injury,
Threatening with feigned indifference,
Sending their paltry death wishes
Like an insidious new brand of junk mail.

You'll be surprised
Who in the crowd will shout, "Jump!"
Somebody's mother will hate you,
A voodoo doctor
Will be paid to pin you.
A gambler will lose a thumb for a debt,
Then bet against you and lose the other.
A father will beat his children
Because he thinks
They somehow have your eyes.
His wife will kill him and blame you.

But when you die two dozen years later
They will celebrate your heresy,
Some of these same
Passing the new myth
So easily across their liver lips
To grandchildren that hate
Everything they say.

An Asterisk as Big as a Ball

the ball talked to
three hundred thirty feet of air,
rising into the teeth
of the bat's echo,
crashing into right field bleachers
like any other Yankee missile —

an exiled hero
circled the Ruthian diamond
to footnote glory —

just down the first base line
the magic bat lay,
like a gun that had killed
its owner.

Henry Louis

born in the shadow of the orphan's number
Mobile's heat cracked
and dried the sandlots
that could not contain
his childhood drives.

summers spent carrying
great blocks of ice,
the orphan's number
carved into the face of a distant mountain,
the color line blazing a circle about it.

when I was eight
I read the Shapiro biography
that planted this hero
in my huge imagination,
then followed him
from beer town
back down South
where he ambushed the HALL.
…
how long now
since Jackie freed the record book
from its white straitjacket,

how long since
Henry threw his nonchalant shadow
over the orphan's number.

Aaron

So what
he played in Atlanta
where the mound
was his warning track,
and the fences drooped
(or seemed to) when
he zinged a liner
that never climbed higher
than a horse's head...

in the field he moved slowly, (or seemed to)—
what is the word now?—*deliberately*
getting there,
was always the tortoise
whipping the hare,
check the records for luck.
You'll find the numbers
were all in his wrists.

Things They Wrote

cannot be written here because
I have sworn to omit those words
from my work except when
completely necessary to achieve reality —
but they wrote them, letters and notes, sent their
mental excrement through the postal curve
till they arrived by the fetid box full,
yet he advanced to the batter's box
without hesitation or a change of mannerism,
propping the bat against his muscular hip
as he adjusted the blue helmet inscribed
with the white cursive *A*,
while behind anonymous blue eyes
the crosses flamed yellow and orange and white
and fed each other across a century of fear and desolation,
the sorrowful critics inked their own comparison excuses
while he was guessing high and hard,
letting the air out of the stadium
one more time,
a stadium now doomed to a steel ball
that cannot wipe out the things they wrote,
or the filth that guttered his phone
in the blackest depths of the night.

Linear History

He comes at the pitch
Like a lion with red mane,
On a line
You could diagram,
With his back foot
The stationary leg of a compass,
He sweeps through
With the full power
Of the perfect circle,
Sending the spheres
Into an orbit of flashes.
They line up
Just to see him practice,
Lines of articles
Intersect with reality
Sometime in September.
In another sixty years
The grass will go brown
On his grave.

Suffering Through the
Major League Record Books

A glossy black-and-white
And some bold numbers beneath
Don't suggest colorful life,
Or great animated moments,
Sluggers with one-day beard grimaces
Caught in flat stride headed
Merely for first,
Enthusiasm reduced,
Synthesized, anesthetized
In dried ink.
All the great exploits
Of diamond masters
Generating this plethora of bland trivia,
A poet must have the fans and their cheers
Or lose himself
In this thin substance called history.

stories of their broken toys

never on a bench with the clack of metal cleats
always chipping at smoothed concrete,
not by the strictest straightest foul line
ever estimated by the cleanest engineer,
never in a frisky bullpen with its ice water jokes
and its Walter Mitty dreams,
never inside the stifling booth with statistical prose
and between-inning hotdogs,

the hard-eyed harrier boys in backwards caps
have left them, squelched them, fitted a rough face
to their memory.
this business, this business it seems
has made of them, men that can't cry anymore,
walking numbers, blades of August grass.

Budweiser!

Budweiser! he calls
between innings, between pitches,
between breaths

The Walls of Comiskey Caving (on CNN)

after the war channel
crab crawled through
every possible crater
of deluge
having shoved camera and mike
into glorious horror
of high tech explosion
of concrete steel enemy flesh
to living room cheering section
of full mast America

and now in the second month of our forgetfulness
this yuppie slick
reporter heroically close
without construction hat
for us to describe the first
shiver of the crane chain
casting a ball now meant
for the outside of a house that
held so many ferocious smaller ones in.
and I am feeling inside out
once again on the vision end of
this satellite signal

there's a brief pause
and a black-and-white film clip stutters
on to screen,
the sweet swagger of opening day, 1910,
before Ruth built,
before Shoeless Joe slipped,
before ivy crawled Wrigley
across town.

The Catcher Learns the Motion

and is often the hub of the movements,
he reads the morse code of the pitcher
and returns the speech of the dumb,

he loves the sphere and its ridges,
rips it from the tight mitt
with or against the seams
whistles it from a frog squat.

the catcher learns
he is the hat of the hat dance,
the pitcher may think himself
the center of gravity,
but the catcher
waits at the apex of the great angles,

slaps the leather trap
on the errant razor
as it spits up from the dust.

the catcher imprints the motions of the hitters,
checks the rhythm of their passages,
knows he must slip an extra measure
at the end of their cha-cha-cha,

the catcher is the great disturber,
can cock twice on his return throw,
spit on the plate, call for the "buzzer"
block the ump's clear visage,

bilingual kamikaze
chattering like a wired chimp,
muttering with silent busted digits,
sacrificing legs
to the varicose crouch and
the ruinous crunch
of the few that get through
to thin armor.

Josh as I Am

a shaking window
on a doorslam afternoon,

your children left crying
for money beer-spent
and whoring...

maybe you coulda
fired a volley to second
caught Cobb
escaping your one-bagger jailhouse
then swinging with the shoulders
from the hips
knocked the choo-choo end
off the Big Train
maybe you coulda...

when fourth of july
meant nothing but a doubleheader...
no phone call from a president
that tape-measured your heroics.

Josh,
I am just a shaken window
on a doorslam afternoon,
and no,
they'd never
mickey your mantle
with trophies from the BIGS,
never even
civilize your numbers
into totals.

The Babe Ruth Syndrome

he had it all;
the smile, conscious
of all his unconscious movement,
could enter any bar
like stepping to the plate
without warmup swings,
point the ole stick at his chosen target,
leave with her later,
having danced to home run music.

Josh, What the Future

How can I say how you would do today?
I'm not so simple as to believe
the ancients could vindicate themselves
against the moderns;
this would be counter-evolution:

with every kid six-five, two-twenty,
a farm boy fastball,
a split-finger dropping a dart
behind the catcher's feet;

gymnast infielders, hoopster outfielders,
specialists, one-inning assassins,
hooded and waiting in fat bullpens,
managers with an eye on the field
and a finger on a computer port.

It's like asking what would Jimi Hendrix be playing now:
you think you know, maybe,
but it doesn't matter.

Josh, in the Islands

where they treated you white,
and the cow-eyed children ran like ducks
around your feet in the dusty city streets
babbling the Spanish that you could never
unscramble...

gallons of cheap beer
couldn't stop the heat.
By the seventh it was murder,
and the brew that night
was to maintain weight,
you told yourself.

Josh, You Were

caged out
of white daytime
of the dark game
without a flash of light

amos 'n andied to death
opaque kingfish
swish through this saltless scheme
    of life

the flare and flame
of a doubleheader grin
all the way round the rim
of a warm mug of cuban beer

Ruth, your pale emanation
transparent
as the taste of glass
in the chicken nugget brains
of bronx boys hollerin'
"nigga! nigga!"
then sandworming
from bird of prey eyes
iceblock shoulders

In Cooperstown Josh
you are
the real orphan
adopted too late for light.

Josh, the Grey and Craven

limping ghost that lingers
along a blurry foul line
between a night with a sky
filled by asterisks,
and a day — dull and colorless
as the few chaps that remember
your boyish grin, now opaque
and in neither world —
not even in Kinsella's dream
Josh, like smoke that floats
forever.

Josh, the Real Casey?

The steel mills could not have shaped
Those arms.
Who could challenge this kind of manhood?
Understand it, acknowledge it?
Squatting behind wild plates
That pointed the wrong direction
At a million different fields,
The grass grows together;
The lines disappear.
The family is at best
An unknown distant quantity,
Occasionally begging your drink money.
Is this how death gets bottled young?
Is there a back door to "The Fire"?
Or does Whitey
Even share his hell?

Josh, the Lights and Distances

Were the two things that never
Came together for you.
The light never really came on —
We will forget the distances
Because there were no lights.

Your career was like the second half
Of a doubleheader played into twilit shadows,
The powerful teams locked
In a sister-kisser,
With you coming toward the plate,
The white sun slipped to China.

It Makes You Scratch Your Head

Dark, straight blonde hair,
Showing the first signs of recession;
Thin, reddish moustache
Curled around the corners of his drawn mouth;
One day's sparse stubble
On his cheeks and chin.

"Would you like to sit down while you wait?"
I invited, as the quintessential desk clerk,
Tirelessly polite.

"No. No, I've been sitting all night, man."
New Jersey accent,
Slightly stoop-shouldered,
Wearing faded jeans and a dark T-shirt,
Medium build, about five-ten, age: thirty-two or so.

"I got to get to Baltimore today, man.
I wanna see my family before spring training.
I'm headed for Florida Friday."

"The taxi will be here in a minute. It'll take you to
The bus station." "Okay."

Lighting a filterless cigarette with a shaky,
Motel match, stinking of spilt beer, jumpy and talking
Fast between pauses.

"You ever heard of Brooks Robinson?"

"Who?"

"Brooks Robinson — played for the Baltimore Orioles.
I belong to the Baltimore Orioles. I'm going to play
Third base like Brooks Robinson,"
He aims a penetrating glare at me.

"Yea, Baltimore's a good organization."

"It is the best in the world, maybe the universe. Did you know they
won the World Series two years ago.
And they won it before that also."

Pacing back and forth across the lobby, towards and
Away from me, dragging tons of smoke from the cigarette,
Such efficiency.

"You know a million dollars a year is hard to turn down."

Stopped at the counter, leaning on his fists, and staring
Straight into my curious eyes.

"So I figure, what the hell, ya know! I'll play for that."

I notice the blue letters tattooed across his knuckles
Don't spell anything — except a stitch in prison.

This is not funny, I tell myself, fighting back a gale of laughter,
Not funny, I bite down on the phrase.

Finally, the cab arrives out front.

"Did you know they called Johnny Unitas the man with the golden
Arm? He played for the Baltimore Colts just like Brooks Robinson
Played for the Baltimore Orioles. They're giving me Brookie's
number, ya' know."

He was making the cab wait as an affirmation
Of his importance.

"Call the airport for me. I need to check on a flight."

"I'll call. You talk. Okay."

I dial and hand him the receiver. He talks incoherently
Into the wrong end, then plops it down and stumbles
Toward the door, seems to find himself as he pushes
The thick glass — turns a twisted look back to me.

"Hey — sometime — ya' know — down the road — I'll send yous
Some tickets — you can come see me play."

He's gone, my laughter unleashed — then shame swept over me
As I remembered the same feeling in elementary school
When the children laughed at a young retarded girl
Who tried to read in front of the class.

Two weeks later — a letter arrives marked extremely urgent —
It contains box seat tickets
For a weekend series between the Tigers and Orioles.

Damaged Goods

He only learned two things in high school physics:
What makes a curve break,
And there is no such thing as an accident
Because two objects can not possibly occupy
the same space at the same point in time.

So as the ball zipped toward his head,
He checked the rotation first,
Then drove it deep enough
To raise major league scouts
Up off their worn out lawn chairs.

Apparently he forgot his lessons.
When he failed the Blackburn curve at 80 mph,
His old Ford pickup tried
To occupy the same space as a utility pole.
The left eye tore loose as the socket was crushed,
His vision halved.

When he took his dream to the other side of the plate,
He could not judge the direction
Or spin of the ball,
His muscles and reactions
Would not work in reverse.

Now he's thirty-five,
Turns a tired wrench in his daddy's garage,
Has a mind that backtracks
To better "times,"
So well that he relives the very smell
Of the first inning of the first game
He can remember
Like it was this morning's coffee.

As his mind winds and kicks,
He no longer notices
The dark space to the left,
Or imagines what greatness
Might have brightened there.

When I Grow Up

Will I hit the bristly curve
As it drops from the guillotine air?
Will I dance clever rhythmic steps
Swaying full-shouldered
Against a gliding, smiling partner?
Will I bury a caught breath
In the water of a perfect crawl stroke,
Calmly swivel for another?

Will I elicit a healing word,
Unstammered at the wake?
Will I discern in time
Who holds the dagger for me?
Will I learn to hit
All the crazy curves
When I grow up?

What I Will Try to Know

The direction, drive, and drop,
The fierce curve winking
Into the mitt and its plop.

That a curve would not break in space,
Propellers would beat nothing forever,
That birds would flap absently
Like words hanging motionlessly
Between mind and page.

That speed is relative,
That legs are powerful,
The Aboriginal grip on an ancient weapon
That slashes an ultimate curve
And only is what it is,
Too clean for symbol,
Too pure for metaphor.

Eisenreich

Into a game so swamped
With superstition and ritual:
Of lines skipped, steps counted,
Clover leafs in catchers' mitts,
Lucky shoes and undershirts,
A wife kissed on the same cheek
　　in leaving,
The exact spot on the dugout bench,
The mound entered at an identical
　　angle,
The strangeness of "around the
　　horn,"
And spastic base coach signals,
Enter a quiet man
Who quietly fights
An invisible battle
With his own chemicals,
The battle with grunts
And facial contortions,
Incessant whistling,
The relentless pat of a foot,
The flap of an elbow,
The twitch of an eye.
Perfectly still in the batter's box,
Straight as an eagle, Eisenreich.

I remember my own struggle,
The pleasant relaxation
When I allowed the flow
Of dove-like noises, gave

Myself to the intensity
Of the urges. Earlier
I may have been declared possessed,
Or a warlock, put in stocks,
Drowned, or burned.
My loving parents defined me
As "nervous"
While I fought to disguise
The inevitable with hacks
And sneezes and funny
Cross-eyed glares, let the
Games and sports grow
Beyond controllable perspective,

Till somehow eventually,
I got beyond it or put it inside me.
And though I never
Cussed out loud in church,
Uttered racial epithets
In a line at the bank,
Or touched people at the mall
Obsessively,
I understand the fiery impulse
Of Tourette's Syndrome,
I know Jim must take it with him
Between the lines,
And so becomes my hero
When I thought
I'd never have one again.

Sometimes You've Gotta Change the Names

Fred Trump was the bad card
We had as a substitute teacher.
In P.E. class he charged at us
Like a loony drill sergeant,
His shoulders always squared and forward,
A hideously level jaw jutted even further,
His flat top and face that combined
Vince Carter with a cocksure Gomer Pyle.
He was in your face from twenty feet away
Which was livable for a couple slack days,
But when he covered for the baseball coach
At practice, he at once became a living irony.

You see, Fred stepped up to Matt, our top pitcher,
At six feet tall, an easy target for the combative cretin
Who immediately decided that Matt, who was not only
Big, but also had the conservative, worried look of an adult,
Was not "with the program." And so proceeded with a
Harangue about his accomplishments as a "hind catcher"
At the local private college and in the Army, admonishing Matt
For his longheadedness (he did have a long face and neck),
He continued, "you are stupid as a mule, and, consequently,
(you could tell he was proud of his word choice)
I'll probably need to hit you upside the head with a two-by-four
Just to get your attention."

We all stood or sat there, depending on whether we were
On the bench or huddled behind this genius. Matt didn't utter a word
Or move a muscle; not Matt, who we all knew had never made less
Than a high A on anything, who had been pictured reading the
Newspaper at the age of three, who was destined to run a
C.P.A. firm or to run a corporate law office.
Matt just stood there, that serious adult look worn on his face,
Fred's jaw protruding a few inches away.
It was the kind of protracted, tense moment you
See when a movie depicts a prison yard standoff.
Those were the days when you still respected authority,
Especially teachers and coaches, no matter what,
But as we stood there, the undefeated seventh grade baseball team,
It became apparent who really needed that two-by-four.

Our Seventh Grade Baseball Coach

Was named John McGraw, no relation,
Built like Bonaparte,
Pleasant, dough-cheeked,
Owl-eyed with dark rimmed glasses
And hair,
He knew so little of the game
It didn't even bother him —
Must have been hired
Because of the name
Or by the process of elimination,
The only male teacher left
After the important sports,
A mild consolation of sorts,
Like being picked last
For the playground teams,
Just a mutt
With hands in his pockets
And his eyes lowered
To kick pebbles,

McGraw was a good history teacher,
And he listened and learned
Who went where, and when,
Pulled his blue windbreaker tight
Against the spring wind like a real coach,
Shiny black coach shoes were soon scuffed,
Toughened his look
With an every-other-day shave,
A man that would have rather discussed
The Civil War or ancient China,
Would have gone on a dig
Rather than dig in at the plate,
Hauled us instead on a stinky bus
In our ragged red flannel uniforms
To an undefeated season.

John Wayne-ing

My father signed me up for Pee Wee League Baseball
When I was five years old,
So my quiet little secure world became
One of tremendous challenge, an engagement
With nerves as I fought my fear
Of batting against a mop-haired little runt
Named David Bost.
David's pitches dangled on the danger scale
Somewhere between blasting caps
And stranger candy;
Many players would leap backwards
Or hopscotch into the bucket
When David began his furious little windup
And sent such dangerous missiles
That might land anywhere from
Halfway to homeplate
To in the creek behind
The chicken wire backstop.
They could also streak
Behind the victim's trembling body
Or pass like magic four feet
Beyond his flailing bat.
For me, it was two years
Of fear and loathing at the Pee Wee plate.

Watching a spring game
With my dad, Curt Schilling
Bearing down on the Braves,
Besting the sly Maddux
With a freezing fastball,
Dad notes what mental toughness
It takes to stay in on a 96 mph pitch,
How younger players today
Are robbed by batting tees,
By leagues where coaches pitch,
How they freak out later
When faced with live fire.

Schilling charges another zipper
In on the hands of a batter
Like a blue jagged bolt of lightning;
I think of David Bost,
The predatory world through the ear holes
Of a batter's helmet,
And nod my head.

In Theory Only

I remember him as Mr. Cul-de-sac.

He claimed the losses
Are just dead ends.
Exclaimed the wins drive you forward
Into the next level
Of probability.

He taught us eighth grade
Math. Coached hard
A game he only appreciated
For its diamonds, squares and circles —
STATISTICS.

Explained baseball is exquisite amusement
Soaring through the pigeon-hole
Maze of applied computer theory.
Something like that.

Pitching,
He let me walk five runs
Till he finally jerked me.
Stomping a perfect right angle
From the bench to reassign the sphere.

Squirming on the long rectangular plane
Where A, B, and C plotted themselves to the left
In equivalent proximity to D, E, and
F at the right, I became G,
Existing in theory only.

Baseball Archeologists

Hatley had
a catcher's big hands
and had he played
he certainly would have caught,
braced in the squat position
examining the game
from its lowest perspective
with small dark eyes
darting like flashy pencil points —

Hatley never
watched the games live,
vcr'd them,
invited the guys over
to study
inning by inning
in reverse,
the coffee table smothered
with stuffed ashtrays
and emptied crushed beer cans,
at first the speculation
heavy as late game drunkenness,
what caused the score,
the change of pitchers,

rewinding the full swings,
the perfect throws,
in three out layers,
our eyes clearing,
cig butts disappearing,
finally ending
with the first taken pitch
and the sober presentation
of the lineups —

when the national anthem sang itself
we stood
the words jumping
back into our mouths.

Charlie Pitchback

arrived in awkward box,
with nylon net, assorted springs
and aluminum tubes
packed in Styrofoam.
was not the Yogi Berra
we had imagined.
our throws slowed
as they ricocheted
from his square heart,
drifted toward their origin,
two broken springs
violated our trust
in Sears, Roebuck,
scattered our line of "pepper."

Charlie Pitchback
braced on squeaky legs
through four summers
of rained-out games.
his bright orange paint
soon surrendered to rust,
but like all great catchers,
the legs went first.

Keith

Ward of his sister, and of that surname,
In mobile home park trash heap,
From Jerry Springer land,
He threw rocks
At the other players during Little League practice:
At blue collar elementary school field
Winning surprised him like a rare gift.
Coach leveled his cross-handed swing,
Straightened his side-armed throws from third
Till he became a small-time Star, driving home
A key run, making the rally-stopping catch.
His face, freckled with dirt and freckles,
Smiled through the pain of rotten teeth
Just the same a sucker stick constantly
Stuck from his mouth and red smeared sticky lips.
Coach clamped him in a regimen of discipline
More and more all summer but never stopped
The pelt of rocks nor got him used to winning.

Rainbow Slugger

The people that "love" you
Whip your butt raw,
Drop you head first
Into a locked-closet weekend.
You will grow up
To play mailbox baseball,
You will apply the geometry of your schooling,
See the flat plane,
The simple dimension of your swing,
A hand flies at the face of your dream,
Your home plate points toward hell,
The extended angles climb
Toward the misty heights of a rainbow.
The rainbow on the side of a mailbox
Explodes in chips of pastel paint
As you connect so perfectly,
A cannon blast against a siren
Against the black hide of the night.

The Only Thing I Could Remember

about the little league baseball field
were the plum trees beyond foul territory
down the left field side;
my brother played there in a uniform that was too small
for his huge body; my dad coached in a uniform that was too big;
but I was too young, had to practice my pitches
with the fat juicy red plums that fell to the ground
in August.
Sometimes, the little kids would sneak a bat
from the dugout, and we'd "play" a game
busting the ripe fruit to mush
running imaginary bases through a hillside of brown grass.

In the family pictures, my brother stands at the plate
forever waiting on a pitch, my dad squats by the dugout fence,
his chin resting on his hands;
somewhere beyond the eye of the camera,
I hold a huge scarlet plum behind my back,
left leg kicked high in a pitching motion,
as near to the spirit of the game
as I'd ever be.

The Kangaroo Kid

Wayne Hollar drove the school bus
When I was in the fourth grade,
Just about the coolest cat I'd ever seen,
His face pocked like a young Bukowski's,
Pipe poking from his Popeye jaw.
Sometimes he jammed a cigar
Down in the bowl and lit it and puffed,
Said he wouldn't get cancer that way.

I sat behind Moose, as they called him,
And he told me stories
Of driving 90 mph to Atlanta
To see the Braves play, was the first
Actual person I knew that had been
Not once, but many times, he and his older brother,
Claimed he'd seen Aaron smack ten homers,
Saw Cloninger hit two grand slams,
Even caught a foul ball
From the bat of Felipe Alou,

Stopped to puff on that thought
While I grew rawer with envy,
Backfired the bus as we swished through a speedtrap
Past the Brookford cop who roused from sleep
Cursed the kid and all his ancestors
And all his future endeavors.
But in his yellow rectangular wake
The smoke was all he left,
Blue exhaust and gray pipe,
I remember Moose for the smoke he blew.

The Fall I Bet My Lunch Money
for a Week on the Cards in the Series

My oldest brother drove
a high school bus I cleaned
on cheap Saturdays

Lou Brock took
the biggest leads
we'd ever seen

My brother, not the college
type, worried about the
next year's draft

Gibson was an easy quarter
ahead and I rubbed two silver
1965's together for more good luck

I asked my Dad
if he thought my brother
would hold up under Vietnamese torture

I was never sure about Washburn
but bet anyway sensing but yet ignorant
of the traditional Fenway wilt

Victory rolled my way in a two quarter
profit I saved along with bus cleaning money
to write letters. My brother volunteered for the Air Force
Gibson got so famous he guest-starred
with Opie's little brother on Gentle Ben

I didn't bet the next year against letters,
McLain or any Tigers. We watched Cronkite
and waited.

The Thing About Terry

During the all-star little league
Tournament, he spent the days
With me, while his parents worked
And we awaited that nauseous
Car ride to the battleground town
Of Kings Mountain where
A certain slaughter *waited* for us.

We dammed the sandy creek behind the parsonage,
Caught wicked-looking crawdads, ran wild downhill through
Sunlight trapped in woods, topped one momentous lie
With another and another
Till we were pooped.

But though I was voted to the team,
I was not stupid enough
To think my Dad would play me
And therefore didn't care;
Terry, on the other hand,
Batted .750 with numerous homers
And the fiercest baserunning
Dad had seen from a twelve-year-old,
Who was my charge to keep "ready"
For the game, so Dad was boiling when he caught us,
Soaked, sunburned, filthy hogs with leaves
And grass and creek bottom clay
Stuck all in our hair.

The Kings Mountain boys were strapping giants
That slammed long home runs
Off our best pitchers, and their pitcher,
The only one they needed, was a six-footer
Who threw about 80 from 46 feet.
So our guys, who'd been heroes all summer,
Went for the bucket on his lusty curve,
Looked like government observers on his fast stuff,
Except for Terry, the crawdad catcher,
The morning beaver, the warrior Indian.

Terry, who was already built like the running back,
The sprinter, the mountain biker he would become,
Kept his hard head in, dropped two liners
Into the gaps, foiled the no-hitter, spoiled the shutout,
But couldn't save the other drowning sailors
In the 12–1 rout.

You see, the thing about Terry,
Was the brother he had who pitched
For the high school and who also
Pitched to him, full speed, from 46,
A slider, a sinker, sometimes at his chin,
Into his leg or shoulder;
Terry came to the games for batting practice
And, like all the other sports that were
Beaten into him, he was way way ahead
Of the hummer, the slider, but most of all
"The Curve."

How Coffey Got His Nerves

we watched Joe on those lazy
Saturday afternoons,
Kubek and Gowdy always chirping
stuff like
"He'd never believe what he looks like
if he saw the film —"
as if he didn't know or could stop
that elbow from chicken wingin'.
Coffey was Morgan-size second base
and he learned the flap,
the twitch
even though he hated the Reds
for smashin' the Dodgers
every year,
and Joe,
for starting something
in him
that he still can't stop.

In the Dirty Ball Daylight

The sun refusing to quit
Till the last of us
Has had his licks —
A dent of darkness
In somber effort creeping
Like a huge hand waiting to
Engulf the fly of our activity —
Yet we glide unpunished
In another sure spark
Of green eternity —
Dad tossing softly back
Darts hurled from his homemade backyard mound,
My left-handed brother Paul
Deepening the hole with his hard-toed delivery —
And me, redoing a level plane
In my selfish turn —
And Dad, surely worn out as the scuffed brown baseballs
That kicked up at his shins
From the red deathly dirt
Back when the world mostly seemed
Like a heckuva place to be.

Touching All the Bases

best stick on the team
could pitch too, was said,
honed smooth by daddy's backyard curve,
carved from the heart
of his ten-year-old mitt,

the fences had edged their way back,
mounds risen as in puberty,
but baldheaded, Lutheran minister dad
still squatted on his worn out
bean pickin' stool
behind the wooden homeplate
that he cut from scrap plywood,
pounding soft leather,
hiding signals from somebody,

in their fake three-inning game
she soon began to shake him off.

"My" Brother Paul

Like blunt instruments
Your ears,

No current of sound detected
Pinballing through blacksmith bones —

Electricity rounds up a sample portion,
Doc says 30 percent maybe,
Into teasing demonic shapes.

The magnetic ends of lightning bolts,
Your eyes, however,
That harvest profanity
From the unmicrophoned lips
Of the red faced manager
Crossing the TV baseline —
Instead of you, then,
We chime our cloudy deafness,
"What'd he say?"

"What'd he say?"
I hope you tell us a subtle lie —
Why share the secret of unheard sound
With those that don't
Appreciate a legacy of big, perfect ears.

Adirondack

the bat that
stroked a thousand
leaping baseballs
out of sight

the one that
had the print
of leather stamped
into its grain

that tapped the clods
out of
fifty dollar cleats

and
made the dust jump
on home plate
with its nervous plopping

the one that
slugger leaned on
in a hundred
on deck circles

whose fat dimensions
were a blurry wooden whip
in his awesome dusty hands

the one that never
got hit on the brand
that never hit
golf balls or rocks

Old Uncle Bob
kept it with his tarnished trophies
in the attic of the house
that burned last year.

Yaz at the Hall

the mark of the blue collar
is understanding
that you are paid for.
free and clear to take
the extra swings
when other kids
are paperboy, vendor at the park.

yes
someone bunted you along
flied deep
and you tagged quick
raced on his long hours,
the blisters and minutes.

someone embraced the yoke
and gave you a game
that you took like a paybook
ripping out contests, seasons,
revealing more of the blue dream

and now today
this last installment
podium to the third row
–paid in full–
so few fathers
ever this fulfilled.

Jim Rice, Viewing the Fenway Wall

they pay you
for what you can put in the seats,
they pay you to fill the seats,
even the lonesome ones
out there beside the monster

they whisper that you can't see anymore,
in the paper it is a shout.
but you recognize the same sidemouthed reporters
asking the same sidemouthed questions,
"why Jim?" they implore in faked sympathy.
then they are the aggravators,
"how many fingers am I holding up, JIM?"

forget 'em man. play it
between the baselines;
the boss'll let you know
when this gig is up.
meantime the wall
could be in China,
yeah, China, Rice,
get it?

Gaylord

I have a friend that calls it
the Andy Griffith Syndrome.

the good ole boys
in eastern North Carolina
have this way of talking
like they've always known you,
the words warm your heart
like back slaps
from the preacher,
so you've got to read their eyes,
but that's not always easy.

I heard Dietz said
that in the no-hitter
he caught three curves,
two sliders,
and ninety-seven unidentified pitches
that required a windshield.

the denial itself is legendary,
amidst all the psychosis-causing
motions:
hand to mouth to hat to mouth to hat to ball,

and later the country drawl,
why I DON'T throw no spitter boy...
a voice that could be heard
anywhere at a tobacco auction
in a place like Williamston, NC.

Ford

He was a kid that worked for us at the motel,
And it didn't take long to find out that
He was a pitcher, was all he wanted to talk

When he learned that I was interested,
That I'd played, that I wrote about it.

He was small, maybe 155 lbs.
A lefty that claimed about 80 speed
And just so control that he needed
At the Junior College level.
His coach had him lifting weights,
Running long distance and promised
Him to make whatever connection
He could for him.

Ford's enthusiasm was
A bright and youthful contrast
To my cynicism; the outness
I sometimes felt around young athletes
I did not feel around this "good" kid.

But here's the kicker,
And isn't there always one?
End of summer comes,
And Ford got ready to leave, now all pumped
For the fall season.
One day his coach calls him at the motel;
It's Gaylord Perry, anxious to get the kid back
Who works in his office, answering the phone
During the school year.
So who calls Perry, I ask.
Ah, guys he used to play with, you know.
One day, Willie Mays,
Another, Dick Dietz.
Willie Mays! I said incredulously,
Willie "score from first on a routine single" Mays, I said.
It's no big deal, and oh yeah, you might know this one,
Juan Marichal.
Next day Ford headed back to the Coach who offered
What connections he had.

Concepción

Today your name sizzles
like a technical term
in electrical engineering,
"human apparatus used for snaring
wild hops and whistling liners,"
where the carpet made it quicker
than dc current
you shut it down,
the breaker fuse.

after heavy lumber
had packed it up
been traded or called it a career,
you were still dancing sparks
deep into the hole,
lasering a throw
to a parade of first baggers
whose wiring was faulty,
whose shallow cleats
plugged them
only halfway into the base.

you, always
the little man
in the BIG RED MACHINE, but
consistent to rally,
forever charging one up the middle
with hidden power.

Staying Off Coke

try to stay between
the peaks and valleys
at the same time
not believing in them

leave the mirror
on the motel wall —
keep the cat claws
out of your nerves

take up a consuming hobby
like remembering
everything you did
for the last four years

write a book
and testify in court
against the teammates
that already hate you
for the book

get traded and play good,
bargain for a higher salary —
just think what you can do now
with your brain out of the fryer

but most of all
don't forget the lines,
white and endless
as the markers in Arlington,
and how loud the flies get
when you're buzzin'
out in right field.

Whiskey Fuse

He had teeth like metal cleats
And a whiskey fuse,
Unpredictable, the explosions,
Unforgettable, if you were
The target, his fists all skinned
By Sunday afternoon
He was betting on the visitors,
Unscrewing the cap
With his crooked choppers.
The women had him anyway
'Cause he could hit
What he aimed at — and his heart,
Wound tight and wounded badly
Was in the games he played.

Denny's Talent

The game was a horse he had tamed,
He rose like a star that would
Make us forget the Whitey Fords
And Warren Spahns who'd won
Purely by making the pitches that
  win,
Or even the Koufaxes and Gibsons,
Whose lightning bolts beheaded
The best decade of talent, that
Mid-fifty to mid-sixty bunch, we
May ever see.

When the mound went flat
And the Tigers dropped a notch
Of their offensive growl, Denny
Still clipped that 24, making
It 55 in two seasons, the magical
Year I cheered for the Tigers–
Braves match that couldn't happen
For all the magic in Shea.

The game is not a horse to be tamed
And so the organ playing, the
  nightclub
Routine, the fast and easy times of
  dice
And cards and games of hard chance
Reared up and smote the funny guy
  who
Would rule till he grayed, slapped
  backs
And told great old stories.

By '72, in another of a never end-
  ing series
Of management goofs, the Braves
Had obtained McLain who by then
Couldn't buck his way through a
decent high school lineup.

Denny could have been a Shake-
  spearean
Tragic hero; he had the days at the
  top of
The wheel; he took the heavy tum-
  ble because
Of his tragic flaw. But there's
  something
Missing in this version of the per-
  formance.
Where's the catharsis, the hero on
  his knees
Or caught in a hideous storm of
  clarity,
Begging for honor? Where's the
  pity we
Should feel, instead of the disbelief
That a man could be physically
  ruined
At twenty-eight? Where's the rage
  for all the hundreds
Of hackers who had the stone will
  to endure
But never Denny's talent?

1968

Was the Year Denny
went ITZ
like nobody this side of the century
with a curve that tumbled like an
  alcoholic bronc buster
and the blazing chance of his fast
  one challenging,
coming up Kaline, Northrup, and Cash
going deep on the other end,
and happy Mickey southpaw
attending in the gut shadow
of Cobb's old stadium to a Gibson–
Cardinal series,
while the world went to hell in a
  body bag
on the six o'clock news.

The Star's Marriage Ages Gracelessly

He has flag shadow
Burned under squinty eyes.
He sings her national anthem of sleep.
The parched death of autumn crackle
Outlives their liquid dreams.

His lies grow big as grandpa's pumpkins,
Letter-high, fat hanging curves.
She has run clean out
Of the benefit of the doubt.

Once she was his expensive glass of wine.
Now she squeezes tightly
The fifty cents of youth she has left,
And he hates her for every nickel
She's ever taken.

The Star's Marriage Ages Gracelessly II — Buried

He suspects
That when the beer runs out,
Anger will catch up
With his ulcer.

The air between them decays.

He looks at her,
Helplessly,
And knows
He is going to hell
Soon.

Dick "66" Stuart — "the you attitude"

Something about giving yourself a nickname
Says it all,
Then when you came into the batter's box
In a robe of flamboyant ego,
And stood so tall out there by first,
They called you King Richard
Though the mocking you missed
Like all the grounders and throws
That gained you "Dr. Strangeglove."

Three good ones of eleven years
On six teams, not to mention
That "ugly American" stint in Japan.

But what we remember best,
Your shining moment of fame
Is that 66 in Lincoln, '56,
How you fixed yourself at the plate,
Two outs in the ninth of the final game,
When a teammate stole home
To win it and, as players hugged the boy
And celebrated,
You, King Richard, punched him out
For the stupidity of stealing home
While a batter of your "quality"
Waited to hit.

Baseball 2045

In the frosty dark
Downtown corner barroom
On the end stool
One with foam pushing through torn leather
Our hero sags over rot gut draught
Greasy hair hangs over the lead eye
That once traced the motion
Of the threads
Carefully timed the break
Cherished the rope
Before it tightened
Toward the alley.
But then through the walls
And the ceilings
The voices
Quaking and full of questions
Claw the sheet rock nights
Indistinguishable,
Whether outside or in,
Murmuring drums
Of voodoo
As constant
As the last inning staccato
That leaves you schizophrenic,
Holding this beer
In this bar.

The Second Slam

never quite cleared the center field wall
and the brawny toss took him out trying for third.
The attempt was said to be a noble one,
though the high school lost the championship
in that strip of dirt caught in the fatal cleat
that slowed his slide,
it was 1-A, a small town where a freight carrier
employed half the population and a textile mill
the less fortunate, where baseball was tantamount
to religion, five state championship trophies to prove it.

Fifteen years have forgotten him, the freight moved out
leaving a shell of a carcass, the wind blowing the remains
through two stoplights. He clerks the town convenience store,
his hair and mutton chop sideburns dyed black, he listens to
Elvis, concealed from the bad trajectory that ruined his life,
holding the hound dog feeling of the first slam, the one
that could have saved everything.

Chicken Bill

He always looked
Too scared to be winning
But mostly was

Everything got to him bad,
And he was forever nervous
For something to do

And eventually ended up in the pen
And on the hill, he kicked more dirt
Than a grave digger

Grossly moving
A calculated mound of snuff from
    cheek
To ruddy cheek

With a fidgety tongue that talked
To itself and a hand that hung
From a stalwart arm

That could somehow despite him
    shrink
A ball of snow white red-stitched
    leather
to the size of a Rolaid.

Travis Loves His Baseball

He's old school,
Throws his beer cans away,
Fears they'll make
Them into bats —

Doesn't consider the brain
As a thinking muscle,
Just a warehouse
For the numbers,
Field conditions,
Injury reports,
The effects of jetting —

Doesn't need a computer menu,
A data dump,
Feels the pins twisting
Certain ways in his gut,
That tell him
When to ride the streaks,
When to dive for the dirt.

Like Dying at 45 with Promise

The night auditor at a motorcourt
In the suburbs,
He has a season ticket
For the first six innings,
Charges to work
On the radio interstate,
Pipe burning
The eighth, the ninth,
Chomps the Ball Park frank
That he snagged leaving.
He's missed so many wakeup calls
Trying to catch those West Coast scores,
Surprised sometimes that they keep him,
He bets on streaks
Or the Dodgers like his daddy did;
For him the betting
Attaches him to the whole game.

I've heard it said
That only the true fans
Come Mondays and Tuesdays,
And there is a smaller group
Distinct in its dedication,
Who leave so many good ones early,
For the hell of work,
Like dying at 45
With promise.

Shuffle the Lineup

Beanie weanie midnights,
Snuffed cigarettes,
Spilt beer
Smells worse than Letterman's
New writers.

Shuffle the lineup one more time.
Bench the slumping slugger.
Toss the brash rookie a dangerous bone.
Wait, they're all rooks.
You may as well be —

The owner says W's
Equal tickets
And maybe one bright day
They'll kick you up
To the BIGS
And you'll know then it was all worth it,
The hanging out here in Loserville,
Like a parakeet on a power line,
Always shuffling through a sacrificial hand.

Winter Siege

Stale forgotten champagne stains on
Benches, overturned,
In need of offseason paint.
Ahead,
The cold empty months:
The regrouping,
The rethinking,
The confounded hypothetical memory,
The tending to ulcers and injuries,

Renewal, regeneration,
Tightening the family,
Getting ready to hide
From tired, friendly same questions;
Let the walls be
Where they want to be.
When you play between them,
On a stage of sharp angles and turf,
You must get beyond and without
To build your own.

God Protects Fools with Curveballs

Going after her
Was chasing
A bad pitch,
A sharp curve
That tailed off
Into the dirt,
Evaded the end
Of my whirling bat.
Thank goodness
I only looked stupid
On the first strike.

Fifth Place Baseball in September

Because of drought and a few bad trades
the leaves have fallen too soon
and the crowd is sparse
and spaced like the remaining pieces
at the end of a long chess match

gridiron battle lines have been drawn
like grill marks across the brown diamond
and the ball follows the fifty
high and toward right
till the sun strikes the fielder
like a peyton stiff arm
and you forgive random rookie
for his bad judgment
for all rookies must be forgiven
once in September
when fifth place is sewed up
and attendance is amazingly over a million.

Where Do You Go, Ralph Garr

Thirteen seasons with the typical curve,
Two to three years of breaking in,
Five solid campaigns in "Loserville,"
A quick late season trade, a child
In an unexpected divorce,
A couple more vigorous spells to spite them all,
Then the fade to the bench on worn out legs.

Where do you go, Ralph Garr,
With your thirteen seasons,
172 SB's, your .306 career average,
Your exhausting work
Before jackpot baseball
Millionaired all these kids?
Where do you go when there's
No place in the Hall for your quiet history?
How could you be twelve years
Older than me? Why I remember
Our amazement at your speed,
Beating everything to first,
More like a fullback churning
Through a quick hole.
That same quick hole
That opens for all the Ralph Garrs
That closes so hard and so suddenly
That nothing is left but the numbers.

Waiting for the Braves, 1985

To have a winning year,
Taking time by the forelock,
Expecting, as well, the muse
To break into my starting lineup,
Watching the days slip by
Through the choking red dust
Of a Georgian county road,
Waiting for the uniformed Godot,
Seeing him rise slowly
Between green whiskers of spring wheat,
Imminently disappearing
Amidst the brown death of summer heat,

Waiting and watching anyway
Year after year...
Because my Daddy did
While announcers come and go
Like bad business partners
And different players circle the bases
And leave,
Never granting an October,
Never a harvest moon.

Summer of '85

I saw springsteen leap
from a speaker twice his height,
land on thick-heeled biker boots in mid-song,
rained on by his own sweat,
the guitar's thunder,
the packed house, the roar,
just a good journeyman nothing more
is what he said…

I saw pete at forty plus
take middle-aged flight,
chest plowing packed clay,
an ungloved hand grabbing for third,
dusting off the late tag,
just a good journeyman the look said
as he turned toward homeplate, undenied…

I saw christopher reeves in the stands,
taking notes…

Entertainment Tonight at Crockett Park

Beggars, bums, and belligerent old ladies
Bought all the two dollar seats,
A flock of hopeless black sheep pressing toward the rail
For a better view,
A terrifying strange brood,
Stooped men from Ohio in checked pants,
Having sucked spaghetti noodles
Through now dried lips,
Rubbing gray facial stubble with the backs of liver-spotted hands,
Their wives lugging the oversized pocketbooks
Of wrestling fans, fishing for Kleenex
To wipe the filthy dusty bleacher —
Kids from the "Knothole club,"
Some in ill-fitting scout uniforms,
Tossing orange peels and spit wads
At the other team's right fielder —
As fate would have it,
A leader emerges from among the group,
A beer-bellied shirtless man
Who flops like a blue-gill just out of the nearby Catawba
Chanting "block that point," and "dee-fense! dee-fense!"
Interrupted by a bird dropping like an artist's
White splat of paint on his bald pallet,
He falls as if shot, curses Crockett and God,
Recovers with a twelve-ounce shot of draught,
Then confronts those Buckeyes
And their shaking liver-spotted fists
Till finally he is pummeled by pocketbooks
And trampled by Hush Puppies
While some pretty good baseball is actually played
Down on the field.

Holding Back

the dam of this baseball/espn thing,
trying to late night my way to knowledge
choose pbs lecture
this lovely eloquent phd lady
unlatching the gate to our latin past
where my concentration
smothers
her words kiss
silent darkness
I know there must be
a serious medical term for this
involuntary deafness
I hear fragments, the fumbling med scholar
jumbling parts of cadavers —

even before
I can click the remote
I think a carpe diem fastball
meeting a veni vidi vici swing.

So I've Got the Class

writing practice descriptive paragraphs
of an old baseball glove and
a discarded bicycle helmet —
they are night students, the typical queer
combination of young struggling humans
that make their valiant stab at
something better than hoisery mill
furniture plant or worse, some organized mode
of franchised poverty/the grill splatter
under the "Golden Arches."

tonight, and nearly always they surprise me
astonish me with unexpected observations,
the faded yellow helmet, old skull saver becomes
an object of this new light, a precious symbol,
I am made drunk in their projected memories, memories
I cajole and pry from them;
in amazement, this glove found in little league
baseball bag bottom, unclaimed, taken home as opposed
to tossing it at the field,
now I find its fabulous possibility
in their nimble description, its valued
place as insert in short imagined histories,
and best for me, those probing eyes
that found the Hank Aaron signature
in the deep heel of the pocket, the
hero of my worshipful childhood, Hammerin' Hank
plainly in gold script despite years
and years of use and neglect.

Pinch-Hitter

It was Scott's poem to write,
And I told him so above the clatter
Of the cappuccino maker at that Charlotte coffeehouse,
Where a gaggle of customers gathered
For the shock of my trailer park poems.

As I poured a Johnson's Red into my butterfly belly
And pontificated upon my poetic philosophy:
"Motion, emotion and heart," I quoted from
An essay in progress, and I managed to somehow note in the drift,
My love for "the game": its ten thousand
Nuances, its million changing faces,
And Scott, savvy Steel Town native
Brightened and fixed me in the trance
Of his Clemente story, how as a kid
Because his dad worked for the Pirates,
He could have met the "Great One,"
Could have held the game program
For the fine stroke of his signature,
Poured some adulation upon this blithe hero;
Instead, he played it cool, waiting his chance
For a "real" conversation by the bats in the dugout,
Waiting a turn next to the batter's cage
Till the season of chances dwindled to
The goose egg of a winter
When Roberto's plane went down.
Just when Scott finished,
A brief hush fell over the room
Followed by a smattering of applause,
And I struggled forward
Through the tragedy of missed opportunities
To read from the delicate efforts of my heart.

Paul Weinman Arrived

At the Casey Awards banquet
In gritty Covington, Kentucky,
On a frozen January Saturday in 1988,

Hugged a motorcycle
All the way from Albany,
Wild, curly hair flattened
Down from his helmet.

There to represent
A photo book on ballparks,
In which he'd edited
A section of poems.

I'd heard about this wild man,
His run-ins with the law,
The electric company,
His amazing record
As a semi-pro pitcher
For the Albany Newts,
His poems that cube
The sex in *Ball Four*.

Paul Weinman arrived
At the beautiful marble
Carnegie Arts Center
In jeans and black T-shirt,
A Neil Cassidy clone
With a cross-saw grin,
A raw peg unable
To avoid its squareness.

At the "full count" of the evening,
Weinman's book won,
And in a voice
As cool and deep as the Hudson,
He made his rambling case
For baseball
As a metaphor for life,
Just like it was his idea,
The muscles in his neck
Strained with emotion,
I believed him completely.

The Real Fans Are in Cincinnati

Even Marge can't stomp the heart
Out of his scene —
In January in Covington, Kentucky,
The Casey Awards Banquet
For the best baseball book of the year,
Hosted by the Quixote of baseball lit,
Spitball editor Mike Shannon,
Tall and business-like
Presides over a blitz of trivia questions,
The like of which you will find
Nowhere else —
In the audience the guys edge
Forward in folding chairs,
Fueled by ballpark hotdogs
And draught beer,
The pace is frenetic,
The questions ludicrously meticulous: e.g.,
The '53 Series — game five — who was on third
When so and so hit a fourth inning
Dinger?
The answers are machine-gunned
From twenty or thirty different guys —
Pause, you lose,
But there are no prizes,
Real fans need no reward.
You get the feeling
That if they could will it,
The Big Red Machine
Could be back anytime,
And Pete might be in the Hall.

Writing Baseball Poems in Winter
or
How to Make a Good Pocket
in the Glove of Winter

hot chocolate spilled on the stanza
about Juan Marichal
his left leg cocked in a high kick,
late-august sweat beaded under his cap.

Maury Wills scurrying down to second,
hook-sliding around the tag,
the tobacco-jawed ump
bellowing through a storm of dust,
his great arms spread like a majestic bird
caught in the instant of landing.

the Dodger faithful
rising from their aquamarine seats
…
the tea kettle whistle singing from atop the wood stove,
our living room windows glazed by frost,
on one channel
the gridironers get in last licks.
on another Sampson and Jabbar
tangle in a steamy indoor arena,
but I am trying to think of what
Dizzy Dean said about that steal
to stick the moment in my memory.
relaxing in the pocket of this rocking chair,
not waiting for spring to thaw my pen.

Ten Minute Poem

it was a ten minute poem,
a last inning with a doubt ending day,
fluorescent light hovered everywhere
instead of one decent sun,
instead of the corny cliché outdoor smells
of the park, the stadium,
we find the wind stuck on nothing
in an unnatural chamber;
the several degrees of cool shedding a faint
drop of electric water here, there,
where a white long haired dog named Steinbrenner
could never come,
because of sanitation or some such lie,
this is the way we kill everything,
by first building tombs,
then lining up our young
like Disney zombies
happy to wait
as far away from something real as
a blade of fragrant grass,
or an outfield freckled with dancing bees.

John Billy's Story

15 in '51,
Left-handed prodigy hurling
For the Hickory Legion —

In the playoff town of Cherryville
Where they truck, make textiles
And play baseball —

Half the county
In the wooden slatted bleachers
And John Billy prodigy

Warms up
By the right field line in front of
The designated "colored section"

John Billy throws hard
Tries to kill the butterflies,
Nervously, eyes

The Cherryville guys in the field
When suddenly there's a thud-a-
    thud-thud-thud
As the sprawling body

Of a black man tumbles down the
    bleachers
And lands near the young pitcher's
    feet;
He sees the heavy man

Has a red handkerchief stuck
In the back pocket of tan work pants,
And a knife jammed hard in his chest —

John Billy has seen pigs'
Throats slit on the farm, has
Shot squirrels and a bird or two,

But he's pale and shaky,
The coach's arm around his shoulder,
Asking, "You all right, son?

Are you sure?" John Billy prodigy's
Head nodding yes, words stuck and
Unable to tongue —

Everything else working
Just the same, he shuts them out
1–0, catches a popup across

First base line to end it.
And the story grows in harsh detail
and intensity
For forty-six years till

I hear it past midnight in
A hotel room high above Denver in
    a room
I share with John Billy, the Division
Chair
Where I teach.

Chewing on Time

late evenings spent like this,
a hanging folder
that doesn't fit the cabinet;
the wrong bullets
the only gun;
I am
gnawing down to essence
the loud fit of the days
not locked to a simple metaphor;
the hound has a heart
for the whole moon;
a cat locks himself
to the next quiet landing;
in my back, the spasms

bend and straighten
my veteran posture,
at times become the whole moon
of reality;
gravity restrains me
on a starry night,
holds me like a sweet chew;
I will learn to spit
like a reliable third baseman,
on late evenings
spent like this.

When Dizzy

became
Huck Finn at the mike
and
blue-haired grammar cops
diagrammed their anger
to an America that wanted
its own language
but was frightened
for its children.

Now announcers
are nicknameless —
emit broadcastspeak

and stars go
rehab and midnight carcrash
and corporate inspiration,
write revelations
in the adequate English
of the Queen.

But Ah that Dizzy
stretched those stories
across the loom of memory
a voice that colored
my first recollections
and PeeWee, the straight man
to
"me and my brother Paul's," and
"aw shucks"
gobble a weanie before
the "Wabash Cannonball"
came rolling,
even crooning
a *bad* influence.

Maddog

The porcelain demeanor
Is everything that gives nothing
   away,
Sure arms parallel at sides, eyes
Focused as the tailback
Glimpsing daylight —
Quick as a firefly
The pitch arrives with a suddenness
That startles the rattled batsman
And presses

Enough leather to echo
A smart thwack in the second deck,
And the plump ump flips
A right arm up
Like a red mailbox flag.
All over America fathers explain
To their too young sons
How lucky they are
To see such a one
As the maddog.

The Human Condition, Part Two

You start the day with an oh-two count,
with a trifling breakfast you choke the bat,
some days the lanky Koufax is back out there
(the Beatles somewhere recording "Help"),
the mist of the memory of the last stripe
still hovers over that outside corner
that is the other end of the bar where you sat
last night, trying to explain to a twenty-
year-old semi-pro player the white flame
that jolted fear into the tight hearts of the best
players of a generation.
By lunch you've taken two balls
the count come even;
the three-thirty whistle delivers you to first
and you drive the great artery with all the
hard breaking stuff—looking, waiting and
headed for the high hard ones
you can handle.

When Wolfe Watched the Dodgers

years he struggled
in a brooklyn basement apartment,
now they would say "paying his dues."
passed afternoons at ebbets
after all night furiously scrawling
on anything
that would receive his energy —
he got there early,
reflected on the echoes
of batting practice shots,
contemplated such questions,
which tilt of the head
throws the fartherest tobacco,
is this the true secret of happiness,
of manhood, of america?
from a high vantage (paragraphs
away from his inner world)
he studied the arrival
of the colorful throng.
through the steamy hotdog smells,
the sticky spilt beer and body odor
he sniffed for his own identity,
knowing he cut a gawky,
uncomfortable figure,
unable to capture
the eagerness in child faces,
finding and loving
this experience, far
beyond the flux
of his great description.

Wolfe, Having to Go Home

For him
The bases were always loaded,
The stadium always packed,
The vendors always rhythmic,
The throngs of Brooklyn
Always the perfect blend,
The gruff and the meek,
Always tuned to a full count pitch,
The ump always rotund,
Slightly cross-eyed,
But fair as the idea of the left field flag
For him,
The pitch was always on the way,
The batter always cranked and leaning,
The hero always a bat crack away from glory,
For him,
The pitches were always wild,
The runners always going,
For thirty-something years,
He never let 'em score,
Kept the game humming
Without letting it move past him,
Never knowing that it wouldn't always last
Another inning.

The Gracious Few

In any sport it's like this,
But baseball is the toughest
Because of the wiring and
The wheels and the strength,
Not just of shoulders and chest —
The season is a slow mean night,
Salt shakered and peppered
On a phony steak, and lit by light
As fake as the camera flash
That captures your false smile —
The excess and the praise
Are as green as the wallet
That wants and holds them out —

Long long ago in a faraway place
You were the one grain of sand
That sifted all the way through
The sieve,
The one favored bull
That ruled the pasture
That ran the narrow streets
That finally made it through
That last proof and out the chute
Into the forever daylight
Of the ring.

July Ballpark Haiku

Hot wicked summer
Against the fat man's belly
Budweiser can sweats

Under the shrubbery
Down by the bullpen mound
Yellow jackets whine

Pollen Clogs

The light where it pours
The poem out
And the brain turns to sand,
Constantly rubbed temples,
No genie to pop from this vessel,
Building to migraine blindness
And unable sleep,
The pounding of baseball bats
Or picks or heavy hammers,
Chronic nausea starts
In sweet air, crawling with bee buzzes,
Through clogs of worry
The poetry shoots
A target of clear sky;
The reedy mind imitates
An unseen storm it wants to hear,
A storming of its own making
In an emerald stadium
On grass as green as this hell
It has inherited.

In the Details of the Heat

There is little to know
But the electric number that flashes
After each cannoned pitch —
The afternoon sun holds
The whole scene
Like an orange in a man's upturned palm —
Where a man might sit
In the shade of an umbrella
The heat roils in faint shadowy waves
That dip from the stands
Toward the crunchy outfield grass —
Even the organ music sickens
In the midsummer swelter —
Beautiful women are runny makeup
And disheveled dos,
Their nattily attired hubbies
Are cotton and Zima perspiration —
Nobody looks good
Except for Pedro who barely sweats,
And there is little to know
But the red number that flashes
After each faultless pitch.

Baseball Haiku I

February swing
Fresh dew in the batter's box
New cleats squeak stiffly

Baseball Haiku II

Brown October
No pollen gathering bees
In World Series grass

Winter diamond
Abandoned to muffling snow
Real grass underneath

Baseball Haiku III

Ivy at Wrigley
Attached in losing strands
To the cellar wall

Banks

in the spiraling swirl of chewing gum park
he stretched like expensive rubber for errant throws.
they had to pitch to williams with ernie next.

in the sour swarm of late july heat
toughened fans dug in and hung on
like ivy clinging to the brick...
and there was ernie stalking a foul pop
all the way across the third base line,
robbing the ball from the wild pocket
of wind
then that half-moon smile
retrieving his hat.

in the sugary swirl of chewing gum park,
in lightless late afternoon
those tense muscles hid
by baggy uniform
a force that hammered a ball
through a hurricane
so bleacher bums
could claim souvenirs.

Casey's Memoirs

A different story grew through
The fog of Casey's ancient mind,
The way that he recounted things
Set history far behind,
His unchallenged memoirs
Told the tale of the day
When Mudville's fading hopes
On Casey's shoulders lay.

They didn't use percentages,
They just knew Casey's swing,
The times that he could whip that stick
And to their feet he'd bring
The tallest and the shortest,
The kindest and the mean,
Into this throng his drives would fly,
A much familiar scene.

And so when Casey took the pen
These were the things he thought,
That on that day of tragedy,
Nothing was his fault,
For the pitcher was a monster,
And threw such velvet heat,
He rubbed and cut and scuffed the ball
And was a well-known cheat.

The ump wore new bifocals
And hadn't learned to look
At the subtle dips and turns
That pitches often took.

Why he'd stood stone straight
And watched two errant balls called strike,
But Casey was just too cool
To air his great dislike,
Of course he knew the third toss,
No matter where it came
If he did not show want of it,
Would soon be called the same.

So Casey took a light cut
Or that is what he wrote,
Not the wild and furious one
That Thayer made of note,
Ernest was as Casey said,
A little long of tooth,
And was alleged by Casey
To have often stretched the truth.

The Mudville crowd was never quite
What Thayer made it seem,
They drank too much and cursed too loud
And cheered the other team,
The field was slow, unkempt,
And like the village name
Was never suited for such sport
As our great national game.

And it was only *one time*
That Casey sank their ship,
His was a long and fine career,
He wrote, and this game, just a slip.

1969 — Casey III Returns Home to Mudville from the Nam

Remembering Nam's heat —
The killing and drinking,
He smiles strangely
As one only could
With teeth like shrapnel.

Casey III — Notes from Mudville, Ten Years After Nam

the marines taught me patience
and exercise.
at night I do pushups
and sometimes she gets under some.

in deep night I lie awake
waiting for the alarm.

we are silent over coffee in the morning.
she looks at me like I am the commitment
that unwinds her intestines.

I crunch bacon
and jog to school on the GI Bill,
mutely accept my vaccination of Shakespeare
to ward off all future literature.

for two-forty a month
I warm a desk, work a night job
so we can afford the child
that orbits in her womb.

I wrestle through the jungle of dreams
on to familiar beaches.
the vision of stringy-haired children
living in a trailer with a woman alone
haunts me.

Neikro Summoning Paige, 1987

Old Satch
you warned us
"don't look back"
and I don't even hear footsteps...
though I cannot take
the hot showers
I understand the heat
the same as my nails
that must stay flat and straight
as the edge of a rulebook
so I can throw snowflakes
where you threw pebbles of sleet.

in late sixties Atlanta
they brought you back as a draw,
by then looking more
like an aging comic,
crossing to Montreal,
reaching into a huge pocket
to retrieve one of your
birth certificates.
your age, was of course
a baseball joke,
and now mine edges toward
letters from AARP,
and spring is a greener, harder
bitch than I've ever seen
but I don't look back, Satch...
not to New York,
not to Atlanta,
for I am here in Cleveland
where thirty years later
the air still smells sweet
as the smoke from your bee-ball.

Neikro Awaiting the Call and the Hall

Who would hire the butterfly to steer his ship?
Fingernails, flat and precise as a wall along Inca Roads,
A pitch floating like the slow spin of the earth in space,
toward a catcher with nerves lain raw by the fifth,
Who would send this butterfly to the shrine?
An expensive vote reserved instead for an overhand fastball
that could shatter the finest ash, that could rip smoke through hard wind,
Never this dance of dice in the gambled air
of Charlie Brown stadium in a slumlord decade.

For him, rather the Barnum call of Silver Bullets
on a barnstorm flight through rag lot fields of dreams,
a role for Tom Hanks as a drunk or worse, a Gump.

Extreme Is the Word

In sports today, the crazy zizz of skateboard wheels,
Of BMX bikes, of in-line skates,
Of rugged mountain cycles careening around boulders,
Under feet and between the grips of your knees;
Human spiders suspended from cliffs
And bouncing at the end of Bungee threads.
All that angst and arrogance,
All that gas gone to pure adrenaline —

All that emptiness when compared
To the whole human feeling of pitching
Raised by dirt, rubber and cleats —
If the stadium is a temple,
Then the mound is its throne.
When the arm is loose, warm-muscled,
And the clay in front of the rubber just so,
And your mind nowhere else
But running to the fingers of your grip,
Aligning the catcher's target
With the perfect aim of memory,
And the batter is helpless as a fish,
Now that's extreme:
Ask Koufax,
Ask Maddux,
Ask crazy Bill Lee,
But don't even bother asking me.

Spikes and Leather

when he throws the
high hard one

it's like a razor
slicing skull

the ball and mitt
slam dancing

to dusty umpired rhythms

the batter
is not wired to his music

and cannot trust
his own instrument

the catcher cradles
a quick leather signal

squatting on new spikes
waiting for the curve

to drop like a head
into his basket.

That Home Run Feeling

tired and poisoned by yellow jacket stings,
go for a hard run through the ripe dark July night,
strides shortened, quickened,
lap by ill-lit lap
in rain-plowed sand
that tightens a muscle against the pull of a worn shoe,
circling the pale glow of Little League baseball field,
enamored by the plink of metal bats,
the hearty high-pitched cheers,
circling as they circle a tauter diamond
in a high geometry of runs;
eighteen-fifteen the park announcer drawls
and I am drawn to the memory of my own Little League experience
playing that 60's cinema
as I suck humidity by the round ball court
where rapper wannabes
work their slant rhymes and turnover dribbles,
and a tired backboard shivers.

Leaving now, I consider
the perfect orange moon
hanging for a moment on the light pole
above silent horseshoe pits,
and just for one splendid moment
I have that home run feeling again.

Running Into LP Frans Stadium

Overlooking Lake Hickory
And pointed toward the Blue Ridge Mountains,
What a beautiful scene with its perfect June manicure.

Because of the hills which I like,
And a student that urged me to contribute
To Special Olympics which is where the entry money went,
I was, as they say, "there, man" for the 5K Run,
That ends with a lap inside the stadium at home plate.

I figured it was the only legal way I would ever get on the field.
And so the brethren gathered for the 9 AM start,
And the heat descended upon us, unseasonably,
Mid–July kind of heat. The regular runners that I knew
Said back off, dude, it's not worth it;
In years past this would have provoked me
To self-destruction. But, my wife counted my
Emergency room bills like strikes; I had two.

So I loped on the first hills that led out to the airport,
One mile's worth, no air stirring except for our flapping around,
The sun cut into me like a dinner fork.
I drank water and poured it on my head
At the halfway point.
Ah but the pace was too slow and I worked myself
Into a froth for the closing mile,
To retrieve some face from the event.
Lucky not to walk, I finally saw the stadium
Downhill and ahead of us.

I passed a group of runners in the parking lot and worked hard to
Catch two more, all of them probably my age-group
About to squeeze me out of a trophy,
The one implement that proves to my family
Where I've been, where the entry money went.
Into the gate, I sucked hard for air and forced a
Woeful sprint. One tall guy ahead.
I stay stride for stride on the outfield warning track.
To our left the wall, my fists out pumping my heart,
The heat like fangs in my throat.

I wanted to think of the wall and its purpose,
To separate success from tremendous effort,
But it was just another "thing" there at the end of a race,
Same for the right field line which became the first base line
As I fought to get a step on the tall guy,
But failed and failed and failed and finally entered
The finish chute behind him.

Though my time was the worst in years
I managed nineteenth overall, but
Out of the trophies in my age by one guy,
The tall guy who was Marty Steele,
Vice-president of operations for the team,
I was just another victim of
The damnable home field advantage.

Sluggers, 1985

The hard hitters
Haven't been born yet,
Haven't found themselves
Unrestrained, unfiltered,
ungoverned, unmuffled.

The hard hitters
Will kill with the edge of voice,
With guillotine stares,
Will roll diamonds
In their cold, precise hands.

The hard hitters
Will gamble and rut
Like drunken lions,
Their spilt blood
Will crack old sidewalks,
The refuse in their wake
Will swallow history
As they validate the new truth
Within the swath of their perfect swings.

Radio Seasons

before cable,
radio seasons —
like the leap between
movies and books
so much drama crammed into that sound,
a bat crack like
the crunch of a truck wreck,
homers that hung forever
in the "way back" stage
of the voice, familiar as summer heat,
sometimes your child heart
caught against the wall
to end a rally
or worse a game —
Milo and Ernie,
artists of the lingo, javelins
of their jargon
buttered the bread of my dreams,
suggested the swirl of flanneled movement,
the colorful sensation of the "rhubarb"
the evil enemy pitcher after his beanball —
my saintly loyal team
like picnic ants
swarming a dropped biscuit;
the shout of close plays,
the disgust of "missed" calls,
the same chirpy commercials
wearing the grooves between every inning,
every night —
before cable,
radio seasons,
April to September, invisible magic
in the Air.

Atlanta Stadium —
View from the Blue Seats

late in a losing season,
cameras also struggling
to find babes in the boxseats.

the vendor that barks like a dog,
someone
barking back.

the singing vendor
crooning his beer pitch
on the club level,
kids booing in unison

everywhere
kids wearing the magic number three
like a parental dream

their saucer eyes
fixed upon Aaron's baseball
on the left center field wall,
and Murphy
running toward it.

The Braves in '98
Contemplate the Age Old Question

In the bustling hilly city of Atlanta
Which looks just like Wolfe's Asheville,
With big buildings and corporate entanglements,
The pretty women, the bright and well-dressed men,
The cabdrivers and bellhops,
The hotdog vendors and winos on mountain bikes,
The children out of school for the summer,
Even the money left from the Olympics
Wants to know what it takes to get over the wall,
To get to the top and stake another flag.
And so the question: if you had a first base
And needed somebody to stand beside it,
Somebody to keep up with the Joneses,
To knock the daylights out of the ball at night,
To occasionally balance the team on his shoulders,
Would you want a Crime Dog or a Big Cat?

Along the desolate three AM strip at CNN,
Deep down in the underground
Where morning is still night,
Out by the Cyclorama,
And in the bedroom sanctuaries of Marietta and Griffin,
Hear the soft satisfied purrs
As everybody and everything everywhere stretches
For one more righteous shot at this thing.

After Mowing, Watching the First Place Braves

Late and only ad-hoc at best —
The guesswork and steam
Have lifted leaving
The heavily flowered disorder of June.

Flies and bees in filthy buzz
Becoming the mechanisms
For poems that are all legs and eyes
And simple,

Simple as self-denial,
Instead of this frayed election
To sit and safely complain
About called strikes
And outs at first and bad swings
And sick pitches,
Complaints from my recliner
That rocks like Leo Mazone
And swivels like Javy Lopez
Turning on a changeup
After mowing.

Enduring Nicks from the
Dead Days of the Braves

the little bulldog,
the cat,
the hammer,
the beeg boy,
knucksie,
boney,
the vacuum cleaner,
knockahoma,
horns.

Defiance

Saturday morning YMCA baseball field
7- and 8-year-olds swarm
to the startling gravity of the white sphere where it ceases rolling

On one side a coach swaggers
like a drugged rooster —
tight jeans a baggy t-shirt
with COACH blotted on the back,
curly bushy brown hair,
a thick dark moustache —
clipboard cradled against his armpit —
he slurs a slow monologue
of orders, insults, muffled
and unmuffled curses
to players, parents, God,
umpires, ancestors,
anyone dull enough to wait
for the sour finish of a sentence —

"Ya gotta get some momentum —
That's the gest
of what we're a doin!"

"Come on —
I can't be-lee-eve you let
a girl score a run!"

"What the hell is wrong with yo-u-u-u-u!?"

On field, 6- and 7-year-olds
swarm across crunchy July grass —
the magical little herd following
a punched out promise of a hit to another
and another, a tail-chasing dog
long since learned to ignore
the cockeyed fool
that struts and beseeches
struts and beseeches
like a twisted holy man
blasting the stars above.

Stepping in the Bucket

When Billy's vision grew worse,
He got scared of the ball.
His dad watched painfully from a frayed lawn chair
Behind the dugout fence
Where you could see him lean forward
Then rise up on the toes of his emotion,
As if he still sat at the opposite end
Of a seesaw from his boy,
Imagining he could control
The fate of his youngest son,
Keep him up in flight for a long time
Let him down gently into the ring of dust.

The Last Game I Pitched

Junior Varsity High School
Against a team a little further
Out in the sticks than us.

At fifteen, I came to the mound
So skinny my uniform bagged
Like a goofy clown or an
Ungainly orphan displayed for sympathy
And potential adoption.

But the sun at Burns High School was pleasant,
Our legendary humidity for once, low.
The smells were those of sweet flowers,
Soft flannel, and freshly cut grass.

The plate lay wide as a car hood,
And the strike zone gaped at me
Like the Grand Canyon,

The 120-lb. catcher bulged to the size
Of an offensive guard,
His normally mysterious fingers
Loomed the size of ripe orange carrots,
Calling a predictable pattern
Of fastball fastball, a slider (called a
Curve then) with two strikes,

But it did not matter,
The gods were in my back pocket
With room to spare,
And those Burns boys went down
And down but for two infield squibbers,
Freezing on fastballs, chopping at curves,
Falling into the big sky of shutout magic…

Was it teenage disillusionment, captured
In the throes of peer pressure,
Perhaps the aching fear of easy success,
Or maybe the lack of gravity that caused me to quit,
To throw that last game
Like an unbuoyed anchor from my ship, only
A sunken treasure of memory now.

My Ten-Year-Old Said
He Didn't Want to Play This Year

and the air gushed out of
me
my thoughts swam those fatherly circles
that can't settle on a rock...
and what came round to me
settled in a question so simple
as why?!
like a hard pitch
against his hesitation
in the smoky fear behind him
his shakiness
in my knees
slipped into his solid reasoning,
his love for the stars
that do as they're plotted,
unlike those boy-hurled spheres
in beanball news
passed grademother to grandmother...
So slowly he became me
in my sluggish drugginess
at seventeen
telling Dad I would run
track this year,
a sport that dried his mouth,
only good to train
for something greater...
searched inside for his mistakes,
Did I start too young?
What "friends" caused
this horsehide surrender?

My ten year-old said
he didn't want to play,
in February he knew this?
And I looked at him/me
cleared my throat and didn't say much
till he caught me with
a sneaky smile and asked quietly,
"Will you still teach me how to pitch?"
and I struggled
on to the treacherous rock
that rose up to meet me.

Watching Him Run, 1993

From third to home,
My lanky nine-year-old,
The slightest hesitation
Then digging white cleats down the chalk stripe,
His red hair flashing out from under the helmet,
Bony shoulders bent forward,
Skinny arms slapping out handfuls of sweaty air,
Gaining speed for the inevitable slide
Toward the catcher that waits with the ball
Awkward in his armor, diligent in his purpose,

There is the dust-raising slide,
The near collision stealing a beat from my heart,
Then the gawky ump jutting his fat thumb
In a hard jerk above his oval head.

From You I Get the News of 1998

My youngest kid tells me some crazy stuff these days.
He's a boisterous professional wrestling fanatic,
A connoisseur of fakery and flamboyance,
The harbinger of hyperbole and sixth grade angst.

His pronouncements nourish my cynicism,
Weariness, I pour back against his exuberance:
The homers mean nothing, Daddy, he exclaims.
The old man on the Braves games
Says the ball is juiced this year.
Well, he should know, Ernie's been around
Since the forties, what a baseball man, I add.

I've just got one question, Daddy.
Don't you always? Is that not my purpose
On this earth?
What kind of juice do you think it is?

Father and Son Talking
on a Sunday Afternoon

There is nothing between them that will wake
or cause sleep, no TV, sports or books;
The heat has penned them in this quiet room,
sun dimmed by drapes designed for these hours.

They tell each other what it means to be who they are;
the father explains the gold his path got;
The son defines the rumor of silver that waits
somewhere in the glimmering distance.

The father has lost his tennis stroke;
The son has outgrown the memory
of his batting average. They reach for the rungs
that matter now, their words winding like intestines,

Inward and wallets splatted under them
Like the nests they must somehow fly from.

Life Is a Long Season

Secretly, we long for death,
Undenyingly,
On and on
Born to balance beam logic,
Babied with the lick
Of sweet angel luck.
If we're still here
To say it,
Say it.

Before ten newborns blink,
Before a hundred hearty cannons
Sit in silence
Before one dirt dauber drills
The sweet whine of summer,

Life is a long season.

Life Is a Long Season II

I see the September of my father,
Days of rain on dried brittle grass.
Weight gained from the medicine
That keeps him alive.

March, he was a brilliant student,
Who chose the cross and the chalice
Instead of the cars and the money.

April and May, he was the great
Church softball pitcher who worked on pitches
Like he worked on new members,
Often at the same time:
His field-level ministry.

June, he taught me to pitch,
And then the mound became my classroom,
The point of reference that it must.

But I quit to run, and we took to tennis
In July, Dad played in tournaments,
Two leagues at a time,

Then August, and his feet sallied,
His prostate took to the cancer,
The hospital door, the knife.

All the while, through the whole long season,
Following first the Tigers, then the Braves
With the fanatic attention he gave
To everything else.

Now with the torrid sweat of September
That takes the home run from his swing,
Fastened down upon the days,

And with his ripe October ahead,
Waiting in a field of harvest,
We can only pray that the preacher
Makes it to that perfect Series
At the finish of this long long season.

Eulogy for Cooke Calvin Mull:
I Wish I Could Stop All Clocks

In memory of all those trips to Fulton County Stadium.

The sharing of time and laughter
is the blessing
that men give each other,
the deep truth of real friends

partaking in the daily celebration,
stretching the stories
across the loom of memory.

A man could take a frown
teach it the sunshine
of a punchline:
whether it be those
three tough cowboys,
that greenhorn from Australia,
Big Willie Brown,
or one of the Clydes.
Leaping back
through half a century:
hitchhiking before "the war,"
selling peanuts at ballgames
in San Diego or
hotdogs in downtown Hickory,
the eyebrows arched in prominence,
his head rocking back,
a hand raised for
a warm backslap,
the punchline waiting like
a ripcord about to be pulled,
in this artistic pause,
in this perfectly balanced moment
I wish I could stop all clocks.

When the '49 Series Went Crosstown

Dodgers vs. Yanks,
Cooke Mull knew he had to be there.

First to convince his buddy, George Poovey
To freight him on his furniture delivery to Philly;
From there a night train to NYC.

With Poovey thus ensnared,
They proceeded from quiet Catawba County,
First stop, the liquor store,
Second somewhere in Philly
To ditch the truck — then make for the city.

Huckleberries that they were,
They bee-lined for the Empire,
Becoming separated in the upper twenty —
And Poovey after an hour of wandering,
Located Cooke in a bar,
Tumultuous, in story-telling high gear,
Being fed and given drinks
To keep the comedy rolling.

In the Bronx they managed seats,
But Ebbet's was SRO,
And the boys were packed in the back
Of a horrible throng near the roof.

But Poovey, who was a man of action,
Reached the limit of his affability,
And along with an exaggerated
Scratch of his privates,
He moaned like Wolfe's Gant,
A most heartrending redneck truck driver moan,
Calling aloud to the very gods of baseball,
"These crabs are about to drive
Me completely nuts!"

And as Cooke always told it,
The crowd around them
Parted like the Red Sea,
And they went forward
To a righteous view
Of the remainder of the game.

Extra Innings

His sweet pipesmoke curled
near the top of section 107
where arms raised at ninety degrees
chopped forward to public address
tomtom drums and the rest of
pennant fever coming this far south
to a place as strange to winning as Atlanta
as if Sherman's flames ignited
the streak.

He steadied his own enthusiasm
the pipe sank into the lips of a slightly nervous
smile as Cancer counted his 66-year-old
ribs from the inside of his lungs
stealing the extra innings of retirement

...

Daddy whipped the dark blue Plymouth into
a slanted parking place on Main Street
hustling the boy inside to Montgomery Ward's
where they bought a baseball for 15 cents.

At Lenoir-Rhyne College field the
major leaguers warmed up for the exhibition.
They were huge men in grey flannel suits
that didn't match.
Daddy pointed out to a man that stood near first
and the boy clutched the ball in his left hand
held Daddy's good ink pen in the other
walked from the bleachers through the afternoon
sun till he stood in the man's huge shadow
holding the ball up and moving the pen as if
it were talking for him, "my Daddy said for you
to shake this thing before you write your name
on the ball." The man chuckled and took the pen and
wrote Walter Johnson on the ball. Then he motioned
to another player who came over and wrote Carl Hubbell
on the ball and handed it back. The six-year-old

boy turned without saying anything and ran back to the
bleachers where his Daddy waited.

...

A second year man and a rookie hit back-to-back
home runs. More bluish rings rose from the
pipe bowl. happy signals to the spirit of
victory remembered.

...

The boy saved the ball through the Depression,
the War, two marriages, the raising of his children.
through the paths of his life that turned him
this way and that with fate always flexed like
a whip about to snap but not snapping,
the boy saved the ball into deep manhood
till a grandchild found it in a dresser drawer
adding to it the names of all her friends
at school and a couple presidents.

...

The center fielder ran down the final out
and the crowd whooped like the Red Men run
off by their ancestors, Red Men who had taken
victory with them into defeat and left only
defeat behind for these. He clamped his dentures
on the pipe stem as the wild cells in his lungs
raged like the jubilant crowd around him. The
stadium steps called for all his breath
but at sixty-six
he knew how much he could give.

The Rainbow Kid Remembers Little League

For Journalist and Teacher Extraordinaire Steve Lail

A female friend tells me again
The games, the sports will pass,
Will never matter five years from now.
I agree, to be nice,
But I know what I know
In my testosterone-driven male heart.

It's hard to describe the smell in Steve's room,
The stale beyond stale of bedfast living,
The odor of bags, the sharp sterile smell
Of medical equipment, the pain killers
Sweated out, of air that simply can't
Move like it should when even the noise
From the hallway hurts.
He angles and re-angles the bed to curtail
The rage of pain that at fifty-two
Has haunted him for nineteen years.
He runs a shaky yellowed hand
Through his thick graying beard and manages
A sly smile and, in a voice that modulates
From weakness to solidity,
He drawls out another story for me,
This one about a Little League baseball game,
We're talking 1950s, in which his team
Won the championship, and he got
Several hits, but the clincher, the part
That fueled his passion, that nearly
Brought tears was that his dad and
His brother could not remember
That game, no matter how much detail
He supplied, regardless of dates, names,
Or corroborative events.
Blame the pain, blame the morphine
If you will, but it galled him so much
That we had to change the subject,
To talk instead about some of the autographed
Pictures on the walls: the cowboys, the pretty
Women, the great comics,
Ah, but that game was still on his mind
When I squeezed his soft hand
And left his nursing home room.

Dancing Geezer

At LP Frans Stadium
Where the Hickory Crawdads play
There is a dancing usher;
The stadium is state of the art
And so is he,
A man of at least seventy years,
My kids call him the "dancing geezer."

When Creedence blares from the speaker system
Or funky John Cougar Mellencamp,
The geezer unhinges his act:
Moonwalking, gyrating, with a perfect rhythm
And sense of style,
Performing a hundred uncalculated moves
For which there is no name, except dancing.

The kids love him,
Would never consider who he might be,
Though I choose to think he's retired
From upper management in retail clothing,
That he spent many days in New York City
As a buyer, watched the Dodgers, the Giants,
The Mets, and even the hated Yankees
When he got a chance:
Saw Snider, Hodges, the Clipper and Mays,
Mantle, Pepitone and Seaver.

Watched Cloninger open Atlanta,
Then followed their stinkiness on and off the field
For decades hence,
Till hometown ball came back to Hickory,
And it was enough to make him dance:
To dance for his buddies dead and gone,
To dance for the rowdy kids who bring gloves to the park,
To dance for the women who occasionally share his fancy,

To dance for the memory of all the women he's known,
For all the home runs he's seen.
For the smell and taste of hotdogs and beer and peanuts,
For the magical day
When America was still a baseball country,
Had not yet given its allegiance,
Fist and pistol
To the pigskin.

INDEX OF TITLES AND FIRST LINES